Unbreakable

Cassandra McGee

Presentation by *BookLeaf Publishing*

Web: www.bookleafpub.com

E-mail: info@bookleafpub.com

ISBN: 9789363301153

First edition 2024

This book is dedicated to my mother and my dear friend Michael. May you both rest in peace. I also extend my dedication to my siblings, my nieces, and my nephews. We have the power to break the cycle of generational trauma.

ACKNOWLEDGEMENT

Wholeheartedly, I would like to thank my entire support team. A special thank you from the bottom of my heart to my chosen family. This book wouldn't exist if it weren't for your continued support, encouragement, and understanding. I would like to take this time to acknowledge both my counselor and my life coach. Thank you for holding me accountable, for challenging me to live through fear, and empowering me to heal from within.

PREFACE

As a mental health professional living with my own unresolved trauma, I made the decision to step down from my clinical position to focus on my own healing. While on this journey, I encountered many losses, including the deaths of my mother, my godmother, and my very close friend who supported me through the hardest days of my life. While experiencing significant grief, I walked away from a narcissistic abusive relationship. Through all of these losses that I have experienced along the way, I found my way back to myself. I've learned acceptance, self-love, and forgiveness.

Dear Mom,

There's so much for me to say
I don't even know where to start
This was only our journey to understand
I love you from the bottom of my heart

I understand the effects of generational trauma
How unhealthy patterns continue to be repeated
So I'm no longer angry with you, Mom
For not being the mom that I needed

I'm sorry our journey had to end like this
It deeply hurt me down to my core
To have to walk away from you
So that I can give you the chance to soar

And you did mom, I'm so proud of you
You put up one hell of a fight
In the dark you faced your demons
And walked confidently in the light

I will always remember the good times
The special moments that we shared
Those unspoken moments between us
Where we both just knew that we cared

Regardless of all the arguments and the fights
You knew my heart at the end of the day
So I'm unbothered by other people's opinions
And I quickly brush off the things that they say

You always told me that I should publish my
poetry
So this book is a special dedication to you—
A dedication to our crazy journey together
For us I'm seeing this healing journey through

Daddy's Little Girl

Everything has changed
Since the day that you died
I thought you were coming home
Until God came and took your life
There's so much I want to express
That I don't know how to say
Even though it's been many years
I still vividly remember you today
Why did you have to be so sick?
Why were you taken away?
I ask myself these questions
Each and every day
Mom's got a new boyfriend
And sister seems to have moved on too
So why can't I move on
And accept what has happened to you?
Mommy's everything
And my first best friend

Two weeks before my fifth birthday
Your life came to an end
I remember watching you lay peacefully
In that casket
I turned to Mommy and asked when you were
getting
Out that basket
When were you coming home to be
happy again?
But I didn't know that you were
already with God in Heaven

When You Left

Sitting here really thinking about
How I wish you were home today
We'd be the family that I remember
And everything would be okay

Dad, I know you are looking down on us
You see the estranged family we came to be
Vicious words and behaviors exchanged
Hearts on fire – the burns are third-degree

I never thought that things could get this bad
It hurts deep that we aren't even speaking
Living on autopilot in survival mode
Deeply wounded – our hearts are leaking

Lost

On the inside, she's a ticking time bomb
And she's so afraid of losing control
So instead she shows the world her smile
Concealing all of her anger and pain inside
There's so much weighing on her mind
And she's cycling through her painful thoughts
When everything becomes too much to bear
She numbs herself to keep going
The family is divided and not speaking
The house feels like a silent prison
She wanders like an abandoned puppy
Longing for a happy and loving home
Her soul is lost, and wanders to anyone
Who will feed her the love she's yearning for
She accepts lies, betrayals, and abuse
Because she's afraid to be alone
I keep crying out for help
No one is coming to save me
No one ever takes the time

To notice the pain in my eyes
I have mastered outwardly the art of being
"fine"
As I struggle to find my purpose in life

Scratches

I'll continue to scratch myself until I bleed
Self-loathing and self-disgust feelings, all over
me
No one could ever understand this filth inside
Sleepless night after sleepless night, I have cried
Self-suffocating in self-hatred I might as well
die
I'm pleading for someone – anyone to tell me
why
Why did this have to happen to me?
Why won't this filth I feel inside just leave?
All I want is this bubble bath to make me feel
clean
From all the filthiness plunged in me at
seventeen

And I'm still struggling to make sense of it all
No one to confide in, there's no one to call
No one around me understands this feeling
I feel broken and none of my wounds are healing
I can't heal when this continues to haunt me
I'm not okay, despite the smile that you see

Please Come Home

Constantly in and out of the hospital
I'm afraid God's going to take you away
When you went on vacation to Florida
God planned an extended stay
I hate watching you suffer
Here we are in another crisis
I'm hurting and I'm angry
I hate seeing you like this
I don't know how much more I can take
Before I break down and cry
I've been trying to keep it together
But silently asking God why?
Seeing you in that hospital bed
Is really tearing me apart
I would have lost it by now
If I didn't know how to numb my heart
Mommy, please get better
I want you to come back home
Please get the help you need
I'm scared to grow up all alone

Tired

I'm tired of my home life
Tired of feeling this pain
Tired of all this drama
Everything is driving me insane
The arguing and fighting
All these crazy situations
I run into my room and hide
Trying to avoid altercations
Trying to wait to go off to college
But that's still one year away
There's nothing but chaos around me
Will there ever be a brighter day?

When I Believe In You Most

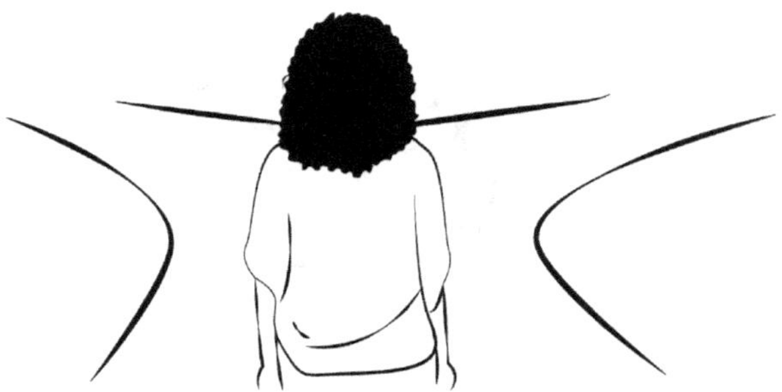

When I believe in you the most
You always let me down
The times I need you most
You are never around
When I believe in you the most
You go back on your word
No matter how often I speak out
I always go unheard
When I believe in you the most
You leave me devastatingly hopeless
Now here I am yet again left alone
To cope with this pain and stress
When I believe in you
My heart suffers the most
But as deeply as I want to
I can no longer believe in you

Letting Go

Have you ever watched someone die before your
eyes?
A lifetime of sleepless nights & silent cries
I'm not ready to let go and say goodbye
But it's only a matter of time until she dies

Watching her kill herself slowly day by day
She's doing what she wants regardless of what
you say
It seems impossible to accept that she gave up
living
At this rate she may not even make it to
Thanksgiving

Destroying her body with alcohol and narcotics
Pain pills, liquor, cough syrup with antibiotics
I can't fathom her being so damn reckless
I love her though, through it all nonetheless

Just don't want to be the one to find her dead
They say some things are better left unsaid
No word in this poem could ever express
This pain I'm feeling right now in my chest

It's only a matter of time until she overdoses
Takes too many pills and slips into psychosis
Until she accidentally takes the maximum
Just the thought is making my body numb

"Please stop killing yourself," I say.
She says, "I'm done…it stops today."
She doesn't realize how she's affecting me
Blinded by addiction she cannot see

I'm not giving up on you...just keeping my
distance
I'll be standing beside you when you reach for
assistance
There's so much more to say but the words can't
be found
I will always love you, but I just cannot stay
around

Forever Your BabyGirl

You went up to Heaven
And left me here all alone
I miss you both so very much
It's hurting me to the bone
All I want is our family back
It's killing me that you went away
I'm struggling to accept this all
Because I needed you both to stay
I strive to be better each day –
A woman you would be proud of
I know that you're both smiling
Down on me, I can feel your eternal love

Back Together Again

I just know that there was a celebration in the
sky
November Fourteenth, Two-Thousand
Twenty-Three
This is the day that you and Mom were reunited
Found your way back to each other eternally

Buried deep within this grief is a sense of relief
Because Mom is back where she had yearned to
be
She's healthy, she's happy, and she's sober
Her heart and her soul have been set free

Both of you are my guardian angels now
Smiling down from the Heavens above
Carrying me through my hardest days
As I'm walking this journey to self-love

One day we'll have endless family dances
But you and Mom get reacquainted until then
I'll be down here on Earth making you proud
I know in my heart that we'll be united again

I Wish I Didn't Feel

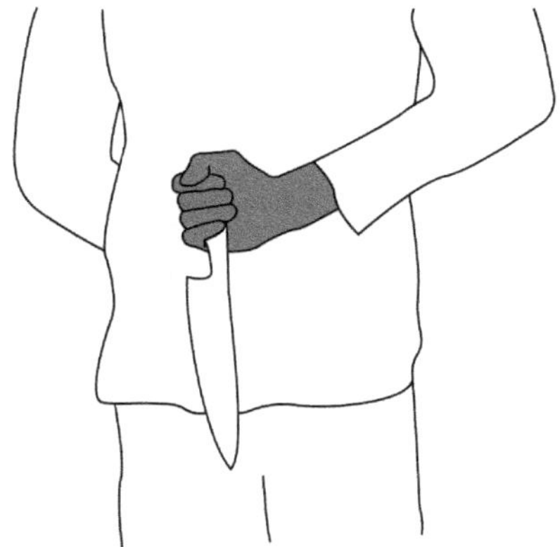

Right now, I wish that I didn't have to feel
I don't know what was fake or what was real
This pain really hurts, but I know I'll make it through
Left mending my broken heart; the final gift from you
All I wanted was for you to love me for me
Wholeheartedly I loved you,
But you only loved my story.
None of this even matters anymore
My heart is already shattered on the floor
I ask myself over and over, how did I fall so deep?

How did I not recognize that you were
manipulating me?
Right now I wish that I didn't have to feel
Because I don't know when I'm going to fully
heal
And it is entirely because of you
That I can't trust in the way that I used to

Inseparable

This grief is feeling so heavy
It's really suffocating my heart
How am I supposed to go on living
When I don't even know how to start?
Why did God take you this young?
We had so much more to achieve
This is all so difficult for me to process
I hate that I'm left here to grieve
I forever cherish our memories
And the conversations that we had
Especially that heart-to-heart one
Mike, I miss you so very bad
Lately I've been living in fear
And truly the only person I want is you
It's been our heart-to-heart conversation
That has really been pushing me through
I know you are proud to see my growth
I live in honor of you and I continue to pray
Our souls are forever intertwined
You went Home on my birthday

Dear Mike,

The times that I wanted to give up,
you gave me the strength to keep going.
The times I felt I weren't going to make it,
you pushed me forward.
Thank you for being my safe haven
during the most chaotic times in my life.
And from the bottom of my heart,
thank you for saving me from myself,
and reminding me of who I am.
Thank you for all the times you were there for
me,
even when you were struggling yourself.
You truly were the greatest friend to me
All the way until the very end.
You took your last breath on my birthday.
Thank you for waiting for me to turn thirty.
These next ten years are dedicated to you.

I am achieving all that we envisioned.
You are my strength and my inspiration.
You push me through each hard day.
You were truly an incredible soul.
So humble with a huge heart.
My once-in-a-lifetime friend,
We will be united again.

A Tribute To:
Michael Ureese Meadows
July 7, 1993 - September 22, 2023

It's Time

Why are you afraid of change?
What are you really running from?
It's time you take a step forward
If you want a different outcome
Don't you know that you are worthy?
Worthy of everything that you desire
You've been through hell and back
It's time for you to walk out the fire
I'm waiting patiently on the other side
I won't let you walk this journey alone
I've missed you more than you realize
Sandra, it's time to come back home

Transition Into My Purpose

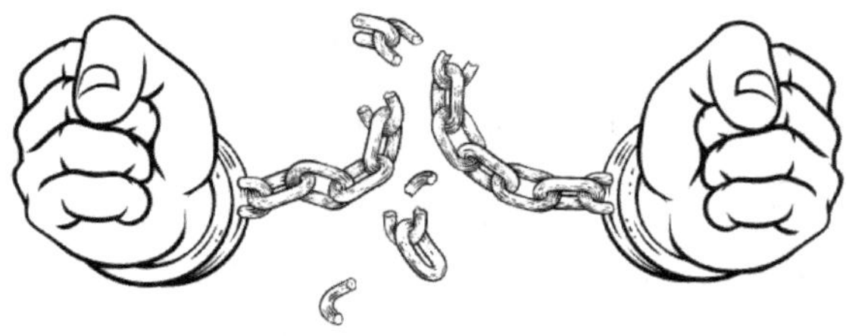

Life's next chapter starts now
It's time to make changes in me
Time to step outside my comfort zone
I'm done living this life so ordinary
No longer allowing others to hold me down
It's time to set this anger and pain free
I'm tired of feeling like I'm drowning
It's time to heal the little girl in me
So now I'm stepping out into the sun
For the entire world to see
I'm happy and I'm healed now
I needed time to get back to me
I'm no longer holding grudges
I'm living life with no regret
I came back ten times stronger
With a whole new mindset
I've learned to appreciate my journey
I did some deep soul-searching
No one can get in my way now
Ready or not – I'm emerging

Dear Inner Child

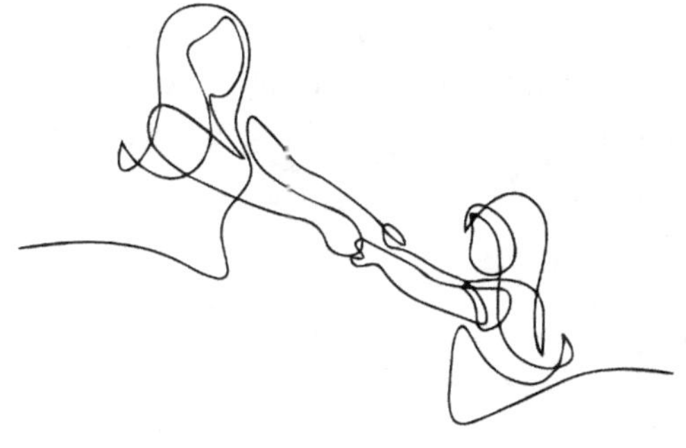

Dear inner child, I'm back now
Come and let me wipe those tears
I'm sorry that I've been away for so long
I'm here to take away your pain and fears
Let me take on all the adult matters
It's time for you to finally be a child
Now don't you worry about anything at all
Innocently, she looked up at me and smiled
Sandra, I'm sorry that you hurt so deeply
I'm back by your side and together we will heal
You let me take on the big scary things
While you rest okay, do we have a deal?
I could see heaviness lifting off her shoulders
As she handed it all over to me
There's a glow, a lightness to her now
An aura, an energy that's carefree
Meanwhile, I'm defeating these demons
I'm no longer allowing them to be in control

This comeback right here is personal
And I mean that down to my soul
I looked Sandra dead in the eye and apologized
I'm never walking away from you ever again
I hugged her so tightly and together we prayed
It's time we both let God
Amen

To My Biological Parents

You gave me up to provide me a better life
Sometimes life can feel like a contradiction
Who would have known that I'd still grow up
Experiencing the effects of parental addiction?
How deeply I wanted to be reunited
But sadly it just wasn't meant to be
In response to your letter – I forgive you
May you both rest in peace

Keep Going

This journey I'm walking hasn't been easy
Some days feel impossible to keep going
Still, I carry on through the darkest days
Baby stepping with my tears flowing
Some days my heart feels so heavy
And all I can do is pray and cry
But I'm so determined to make it
So I walk with my head held high
I know that I'm not alone on this journey
My angels come each time that I call
They give me the strength to keep going
Reminding me God will never let me fall
Some days I feel like everything is falling apart
Some days it's hard to tell if I'm even growing
Some days I feel that I am drowning in grief
But in spite of it all - every day I keep going

You Did Not Break Me

The hardest pill for me to swallow
Was that you didn't feel anything for me
When I felt everything wholeheartedly
Every special moment I thought we shared
Were manipulated to love-bomb me
You sought me out and you preyed on me
You pretended to love me and you
Took advantage of my vulnerability
You took advantage of my heart
Despite you knowing my life story
You created a false sense of trust
A false sense of safety
But you don't get the satisfaction
Of living in my head rent-free
Let me make it clear to you
That you did not break me.

I Am

I am the child of addicted parents
There's no doubt that they loved me
I accepted them for who they were
So that I could set my own heart free

I am a domestic violence survivor
I no longer dim my own light
I recognize early warning signs now
So that I continue to shine bright

I am a survivor of sexual assault
I stand confidently in my own skin
No longer feeling disgust or filth inside
I've learned to love myself from within

I am a survivor of narcissistic abuse
And I give myself full permission
To walk away when it doesn't feel right
I've learned to trust my own intuition

I am a beautiful courageous woman
With a past that no longer defines me
Regardless of what anyone else thinks
I love myself unapologetically